Contents

1 Going places

Today we are used to travelling from place to place or country to country. We can see the world by plane or television.

For many people this is new. Read what Richard's grandma told him about her family in the past.

❝ My family have lived in the same village for as long as we can remember. Our surname was Horbury. This is also the name of a small town nearby. So perhaps our ancestors have lived round here for hundreds of years.

When I was a girl most people didn't travel far outside our village. I was eighteen before I went to Leeds. It was only 15 miles [that's about 24 kilometres] away! ❞

But this was not the same for everyone. Some families did make long journeys. When they did, their lives changed. Over a thousand years ago, Viking people from Norway and Sweden left their homes and came to live in Britain. Richard's ancestors could have been Vikings, but no one in his family can remember it.

Other families made long journeys in more recent times. They can still remember them. Look at the family memories of three of Richard's friends.

Muzahir's story

❛ My grandfather says that long ago his family lived in India. About eighty years ago, they went to East Africa to work. My Mum was born there, in Kenya. ❜

Christina's story

❛ My grandad was born in Poland. When World War Two started, he and his family were taken prisoner and sent to Russia. They were split up and sent to different places. Later they were set free. My grandad travelled over a thousand miles looking for the others. Then they came to live in England. ❜

Elizabeth's story

❛ My Mum and Dad were born in the Caribbean. They came to Britain in the 1960s. I think that long ago their ancestors travelled from West Africa to the Caribbean. ❜

2 Elizabeth's story

Elizabeth talked about two long journeys made by her family in the past.

About thirty years ago, her parents left their home in the Caribbean and came to live in Britain.

Long before that, her ancestors had lived in West Africa. At some time they left their homes and made a long sea voyage to the Caribbean.

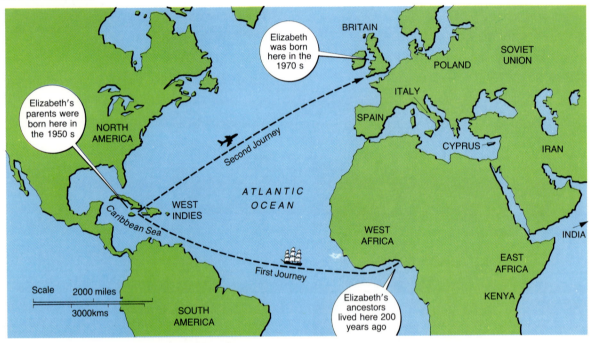

Two long journeys made by Elizabeth's family

Map labels:
- BRITAIN
- Elizabeth was born here in the 1970s
- SOVIET UNION
- POLAND
- ITALY
- Elizabeth's parents were born here in the 1950s
- NORTH AMERICA
- SPAIN
- CYPRUS
- IRAN
- Second Journey
- ATLANTIC OCEAN
- WEST INDIES
- Caribbean Sea
- WEST AFRICA
- INDIA
- EAST AFRICA
- First Journey
- Elizabeth's ancestors lived here 200 years ago
- KENYA
- Scale 2000 miles 3000kms
- SOUTH AMERICA

It's your turn now

In this book you are going to be Time Detectives. You will look back in time and find out more about the journeys made by Elizabeth's family.

You will have to look at many different kinds of evidence to answer these important questions:

1 Why did Elizabeth's family make such long journeys?
2 In what ways did their lives change because of these journeys?
3 What things in their lives stayed the same?

Look at page 5. How many different kinds of evidence can you see?

Memories of people who lived long ago

Pictures drawn by people long ago

Extracts from old newspapers and business records

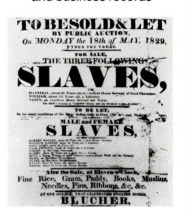

Memories of people alive today

Photographs

Extracts from modern newspapers

3 Village people

Elizabeth said that long ago her ancestors lived in West Africa. Two hundred years ago, this land was ruled by African kings like the kings of Benin and Ashante. Inside their kingdoms there were many different peoples – the Ibo, the Coromantee, and others. Each of these had their own language and way of life.

Elizabeth's ancestors could have been Ibo people. We know how the Ibo people lived thanks to a boy called Olaudah Equiano. He was born about 250 years ago. Later, he wrote down his memories of his childhood in West Africa.

Olaudah was born in a village in the kingdom of Benin. His village was in the forest a long way from the sea. He had five brothers and one sister, but all the people in the village were his relatives.

Olaudah Equiano

You can see his memories of his family and his village on pages 7–9.

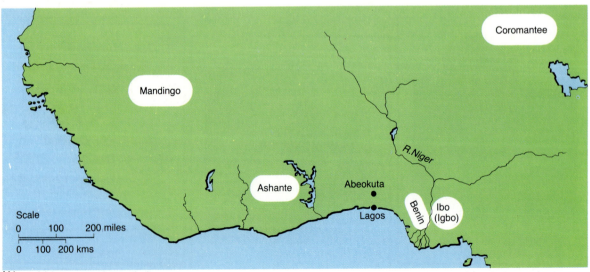

West Africa: people and places

Living

❝ Each family had its own piece of ground surrounded by a wall. Inside were their houses …. ❞

Dressing

❝ Men and women dressed almost the same, but our women wore gold jewellery on their arms and legs. Our people were very clean. This was part of our religion. We made our own perfumes and both men and women used these. ❞

Olaudah's family compound

Deciding

❛ Our village was a long way from the capital of Benin, so the king had little say in our lives. In our village we made our own decisions. My father was one of the chiefs or elders. They settled quarrels and punished crimes.

We had wise men who calculated the time and saw into the future. They were also our doctors and were good at healing wounds. ❜

Fighting

❛ There were many battles between the different peoples. We had many weapons – guns, bows, swords and shields. Everyone was taught to use the weapons. Even our women were warriors.

After a battle, the warriors would share out the prisoners. Some were sold to traders in exchange for guns, beads and dried fish. The rest we kept as our slaves. But our slaves did no more work than their masters. Their food, clothes and houses were nearly the same as ours. ❜

Working

❛ Farming was our main work. We all did our share. All the neighbours used to go to work in the fields together. Our land was very rich and we grew all kinds of vegetables: plantains, yams, maize, also cotton and tobacco. Our women made the cotton into cloth. They also made pottery. ❜

Believing

❛ We believed there was a god who made all things and lived in the sun. Our people also believed that the spirits of dead relatives were always near, guarding us from our enemies. Before eating, they would put some meat and drink on the ground to thank their spirit relatives. ❜

Celebrating

❛ All our great events – like weddings –
were celebrated with dancing, music and
singing. We had many musical
instruments – especially drums of
different kinds. ❜

It's your turn now

1 From a modern atlas, find
out what the countries of
West Africa are today.

Now, imagine that you lived in Olaudah's
village.

2 In groups, draw and paint pictures
showing a typical day in the village.
Then put them together on the wall to
make a wall frieze.

3 Write or tape a conversation with a
trader telling him about your family
and your village.

4 Capture!

When he was eleven years old, something happened which changed Olaudah's life. He started on a long journey which took him far from his family, his village and Africa. This was the same journey that Elizabeth's ancestors made.

Why did he go? In what ways did his life change? Read Olaudah's memories and find out.

❝ One day, when all our neighbours had gone to the fields, two men and a woman got over our wall. They grabbed my sister and me and carried us into the forest.

After two days, my sister was sold. I cried all the time and wouldn't eat. Then the traders took me far from my village. Sometimes they carried me on their shoulders when I was tired. ❞

1

2

❝ I was sold to a goldsmith. I worked his bellows, fed chickens and fetched water. My master had two wives. They treated me well and did all they could to comfort me. But I missed my mother so much and tried to escape. ❞

3

❝ After a time I was sold again to traders who took me to a town. There a merchant bought me for 172 white shells. Two or three days later, a widow came to dinner. She bought me as a playmate for her son. I was very happy for a while. ❞

4

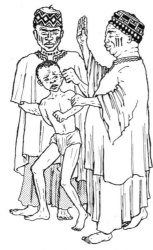

❝ Then one morning my life changed again very suddenly. I was woken up and sold to Africans who spoke a different language. They also had different customs. They didn't wash their hands before eating. They cooked in iron pots. They scarred their faces. I had dreamed of happiness. Now I met cruelty. ❞

5

❝ I was sold to people who lived in canoes on a large river. I had never seen any water bigger than a pond before. But my surprise was mixed with fear when I was put in a canoe. We travelled down river for many weeks until we reached the coast. ❞

5 Human cargo

Olaudah had already seen many strange and frightening things before he got to the coast. But none was as frightening as the thing he now saw.

A sailor on a slave ship

❛ The first thing I saw was the sea and a ship. These filled me with astonishment. I asked some of my countrymen how the ship could go. They told me there were cloths put on the masts.

My amazement turned to terror when I was taken on board. On deck, I met the crew – white men with horrible looks, red faces and loose hair.

Below deck, I saw many black people chained together. Their faces were full of misery and sorrow. I was quite overcome with horror. I saw I had lost all chance of getting back to the shore. I even wished to be a slave in my own country again. ❜

Captives in the hold

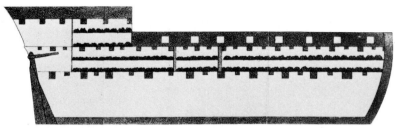

Plan of a slave ship showing 'close packing'

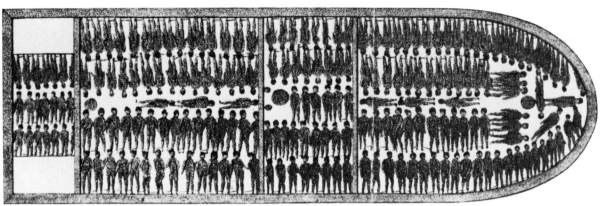

Olaudah soon discovered that the white men were slave traders from faraway countries in Europe like England or France. The ship was going to take Olaudah and the other slaves across the sea to be sold in the West Indies (the European name for the Islands of the Caribbean).

But how had the traders got so many slaves? A French slave trader who came to West Africa between 1678 and 1682 gives us the answer:

❝ The slave trade is the business of African kings and merchants. When there are wars between the different peoples, the kings take captives. Europeans bring different goods to exchange for these captives: guns, rum, copper pots, knives and blue cloth. ❞

It's your turn now

Look carefully at the picture of the captives packed in the hold of the ship. The average slave ship was 30 metres long and 7.5 metres wide.

1 Count how many captives were packed in this hold.

2 Mark off a corner of your classroom or school hall, 5 metres × 1.5 metres.

a How many people can you fit in, lying down or sitting?
b How long can you stay in that position without feeling uncomfortable?
c Imagine you are staying there on a moving ship for ten weeks.
Write a list of the words which describe how you feel.

6 The voyage

The voyage from West Africa to the West Indies lasted about ten weeks. How were Elizabeth's ancestors and the other captives treated?

Opposite, you can see evidence written by the crew and captives of some slave ships. First read what Captain Crow had to say in 1830 about the slaves on his ship. Then read the evidence about other ships.

Right: Captain Crow

Below: **Exercise** (See table opposite). Sometimes slaves were made to dance

CAPTAIN CROW'S STORY	EVIDENCE ABOUT OTHER SHIPS
Food	**Food**
"At 9.00 slaves were given clean spoons to eat their breakfast. 12.00 A meal of bread and coconuts was served. 18.00 The main meal of the day was served."	"We had nothing to eat but yams thrown amongst us. We had hardly enough to keep us alive." (*A slave, as quoted by a ship's surgeon*)
Keeping clean	**Keeping clean**
"8.00 Slaves were given water to wash, lime juice and sticks for cleaning their teeth. 11.00 They washed their bodies and rubbed them with oil. 11.00 Their rooms were cleaned with frankincense and lime juice."	"We sweated a lot because we were so hot and crowded. The smell of our bodies in the air was terrible." (*Olaudah Equiano, 1756*) "The crew smoked the ship with tar and tobacco for two hours. Afterwards they washed it with vinegar." (*Captain John Newton, slave trader 1750–54*)
Exercise	**Exercise**
"In the evening we liked the slaves to dance and sing. The men played and sang while the women made ornaments with their beads."	"The captain says that exercise is important for their health. Sometimes slaves are made to dance on deck. If they are slow they are whipped." (*A seaman on board a slave ship*) "We often went many days without air. Many a time we nearly suffocated." (*Olaudah Equiano, 1756*)
Sickness	**Sickness**
"Sick slaves were given nourishing soup made from chicken or lamb."	"The negroes were kept in the hold. This brought on an eye disease which caused blindness. When we reached the West Indies, thirty-nine blind negroes were thrown into the sea." (*A 12-year-old boy passenger on a slave ship writing to his mother, 1819*)

It's your turn now

1 How is Captain Crow's story different from the other evidence?

2 Why might Captain Crow have treated his slaves well?

3 Do you think that all these people are telling the truth? Explain your answer carefully.

Did you find it hard to decide whether the slaves were treated well or badly on the voyage? Here is more evidence which might help you to solve this problem.

A The reaction of the slaves

Many slaves tried to kill themselves. Others tried to revolt against their captains.

❛ Many of the negroes refused to eat. I have seen glowing coals put near their lips. They were told they would have to swallow the coals if they did not eat. ❜

(*A ship's surgeon*)

❛ Seeing that the crew were sick and weak, some slaves planned a revolt. They tore off their chains and attacked our men. When we fired at them, some jumped overboard and drowned themselves. ❜

(*A sailor on a slave ship, 1700*)

A slave revolt on board ship

B   The fight to stop the slave trade

By the 1780s some people in Britain were trying to persuade Parliament to stop the slave trade. One man, Thomas Clarkson, spent several years visiting the docks of London, Liverpool and Bristol collecting evidence about the treatment of slaves and sailors on the slave ships. Captains like John Newton, who had become a Christian preacher, gave evidence against the slave trade.

Other men were making a great deal of money from the slave trade and the slave plantations. William Beckford, Lord Mayor of London, earned £150,000 per year. Captains like Captain Crow gave evidence in favour of the slave trade.

The struggle to abolish the slave trade was not successful until 1833.

C The life of the sailors

In 1787 eighty-one slave ships left Liverpool for West Africa. They carried over 3,000 sailors. Less than half the sailors came back to Liverpool. What happened to the missing men?

624 died. The reasons were:

a Poor food. Each day the sailors were given:

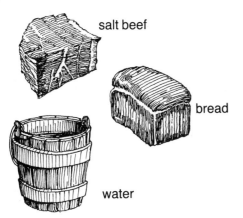

salt beef

bread

water

They had no fresh fruit.

b Diseases like scurvy, caused by poor food and bad conditions on board ship.

c Accidents or cruel punishments.

❛ I saw one white man whipped so badly that he died. ❜

(*Olaudah Equiano*)

Over a thousand sailors ran away when they reached Africa or the West Indies. They preferred a strange, foreign land to the return voyage to Liverpool.

The opponents of the slave trade had cameos like this made

It's your turn now

1 Why were ships' captains worried if slaves refused to eat?

2 What were conditions like for sailors on most ships?

3 From the evidence in A, B and C, do you believe Captain Crow's evidence? Think about your answer carefully and use what you have read to support what you have to say.

4 What other evidence would you like to see to help you decide finally whether Captain Crow's story is true or not?

7 Looking back

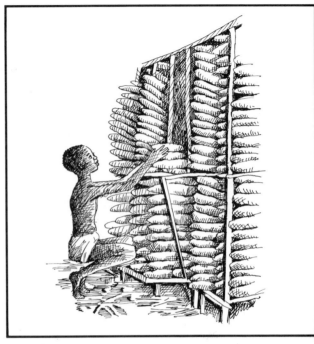

Olaudah's life changed suddenly when he was eleven years old. The pictures show some of the things that happened to him. Look at them carefully.

It's your turn now

1 a Make a list of the things Olaudah saw for the first time after he was captured.
  b Explain how he felt.

2 a In what ways was his life different when he became a slave in his own country?
  b What things stayed the same? Write your answers in a grid like this:

Things that changed	Things that stayed the same
1	1
2	2
3	3

3 a One of these pictures shows something that did *not* happen to Olaudah. Which one is it? How did you know?
  b What can we tell about slave traders from this picture?

4 When Olaudah was sold to white slave traders and taken on board ship he said, "I even wished to be a slave in my own country again". Can you explain why he said this?

5 Imagine that you are one of Elizabeth's ancestors. Write, draw or tape the story of how you came to be a captive on a slave ship. Some of your experiences may be the same as Olaudah's but some will be different.

8 Jamaica

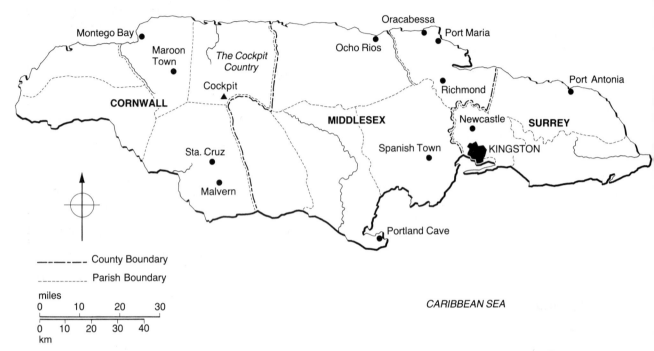

Montego Bay
Maroon Town
The Cockpit Country
Cockpit
CORNWALL
Oracabessa
Ocho Rios
Port Maria
Richmond
Port Antonia
Newcastle
MIDDLESEX
SURREY
Sta. Cruz
Malvern
Spanish Town
KINGSTON
Portland Cave

_____ County Boundary
------- Parish Boundary
miles
0   10   20   30
0 10 20 30 40
km

CARIBBEAN SEA

The island of Jamaica

Jamaica is one of the group of islands in the Caribbean Sea between North and South America, which the Europeans called the West Indies. Elizabeth's parents and grandparents were born there. So the ship carrying their ancestors from West Africa probably landed there.

The first people to live on Jamaica were the Arawak Indians. They gave the island its name – Xaymaca. Later, it was conquered by Europeans – first the Spanish then, in 1655, the British. British people came out to live in Jamaica and set up large sugar plantations. Sugar and rum (a drink made from sugar) were shipped back to Britain and sold at a good profit. The English planters (plantation owners) became very rich.

In the early days, Arawak Indians worked on the plantations. But too many died from European diseases and over-work. So the plantation owners began to look around for other workers. They decided Africans would be best because they were strong and used to working in the fields in a hot climate.

Of course Elizabeth's ancestors knew none of this. Their future was still a mystery to them when they reached Jamaica.

Read Olaudah's memories of his arrival in the West Indies.

❝ When we anchored, many merchants came on board ship. They examined us in groups and made us jump about. We thought we should be eaten by these ugly men. We were all frightened and trembling. All that night, people were crying. In the end, the white people got old slaves from the land to calm us down. They told us we were not to be eaten, but were going to work. Soon we would go on land where we would see many other Africans.

After a few days, we were sold to the plantation owners. The buyers rushed to choose the slaves they liked best. Families and friends were separated. Most of them never saw each other again. ❞

It's your turn now

1 Look carefully at the map of Jamaica.
   a Find at least four Spanish place-names.
   b Find at least four English place-names.
   c How big is the island? Use the scale on the map to help you work this out.

2 Look at the picture of the African mother at the slave sale.
   a Describe how she might have felt at first, as she arrived in Jamaica.
   b Now describe how she might have felt later, at the slave sale.

A slave auction

9 The plantation

After the sale, slaves like Elizabeth's ancestors were taken off to the plantation. Olaudah wrote little about this. Most of our evidence comes from the planters or their British visitors.

Below, you can see some evidence about plantations.

A Plan of a plantation

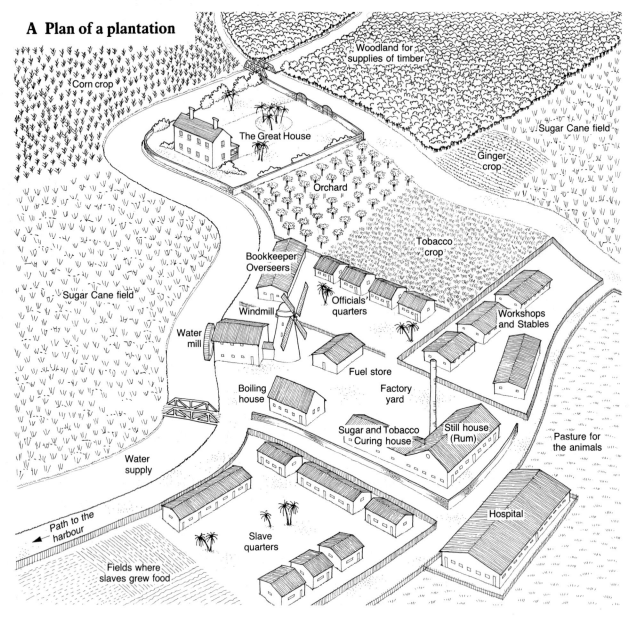

B Life in the slave quarters

❛ The floor of the slave cottage is earth. They have little furniture. The slaves have land to grow their own food. Their master gives them as much salt fish, maize and potatoes as he thinks they need. ❜

(Evidence given to an enquiry by the British Parliament, 1788)

C Life in the Great House

❛ Europeans become lazy, caring only about eating, drinking and amusing themselves. They dine at four. Then they have a nice walk in the garden. The gentlemen play bowls and the young people swing. ❜

(Lady Nugent, wife of the Governor-General of Jamaica, 1801–5)

D Cartoons showing a planter's life

 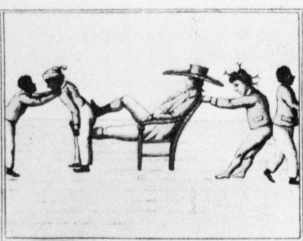

It's your turn now

1 Look at the plan of the plantation.
   a Why do you think the slave quarters are so far from the Great House and the woodland?
   b Why are the slave quarters so close to the factory and the fields?

2 Imagine you are one of Elizabeth's ancestors.
   a Explain how life in the slave quarters is different from life in your African village.
   b Explain how life in your quarters is different from life in the Great House.

10 Plantation work

From dawn till dusk, six and a half days a week, Elizabeth's ancestors worked on the plantation. At harvest-time they worked even longer. Below, you can see evidence of their work.

It's your turn now

1 Look at the account.
   a There were 304 slaves altogether. Where did most of them work?
   b Do the people listed add up to 304? What do you think happened to the others?

2 Now look at the pictures. Where would you have preferred to work and why?

3 Compare work on a plantation with work in an African village. Use a grid to help you.

The account of slaves on Braco Estate, Jamaica, 1796

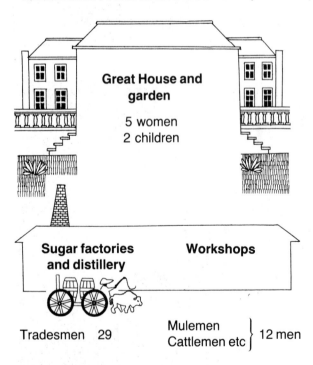

Great House and garden

5 women
2 children

Sugar factories and distillery   **Workshops**

Tradesmen   29   Mulemen
                        Cattlemen etc } 12 men

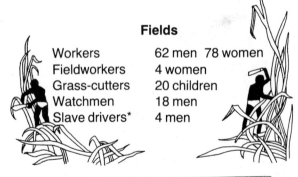

Fields

Workers	62 men 78 women
Fieldworkers	4 women
Grass-cutters	20 children
Watchmen	18 men
Slave drivers*	4 men

Hospital

Midwife	1 woman
Nurse	1 woman
Sick	32
Too old to work	7

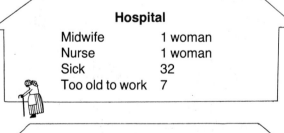

Slave quarters

23 children under 3 who did not work

* Slave drivers carried whips to make sure that the slaves in their gang worked hard

Working in the Great House

Working in the fields

A slave driver

The sugar boiling house

11 Seasoning

The planter called the Africans' first three years in the West Indies "the seasoning time". During the seasoning time, he tried to make them forget Africa and their old way of life. Instead, he wanted them to settle down to a new way of life as obedient slaves.

It's your turn now

Look at the evidence.

1 Make a list of the methods the planter used:
a to make his captives forget Africa;
b to make them obedient slaves.
Some points could go in both lists.
2 Imagine that you are a planter. Explain why you think seasoning is important.

A List of slaves from Island Estate, Jamaica, 1778

Name	African Tribe	Description	Value
Isaac	Ibo	Seven years in this country	£140
Quacow	Coromantee	Four years in this country, blind in one eye	£120
Greenwich	Creole	Born on the estate, about twelve years old	£140
Peter	Mandingo	10 years old, sick with yaws and with poor eyesight	£50
Nelly	Ibo	Several years in this country	£95
Rose	Ibo	Old, many years in this country	£80
Queen	Coromantee	Four years in this country	£100
Bellah	Nago	Seasoned	£90
Luckie	Mandingo	Young, two years in this country	£60
Beck	Congo	Young, two years in this country	£70

B Why drums were forbidden

❛ At first the Africans were allowed to use trumpets and drums made of a hollow tree, but as they used these in their wars at home in Africa, it was thought to be a call to rebellion. So drums were forbidden. ❜

(Sir Hans Sloane, a European visitor, 1707)

C Clothes

❛ The Negroes ought to be given clothes twice a year as follows:
Men – a jacket, hat, shirt and trousers.
Women – a jacket, hat, handkerchief, petticoat and wrapper. ❜

(Evidence given to an enquiry by the British Parliament, 1788)

D Punishments

The treadmill

12 Rebels and runaways

During the seasoning time, the planter tried to turn his African captives into obedient slaves. Did he succeed?

First, look at evidence A below.

A A plantation owner's view, 1815–17

❛ I never saw so many people who were so happy. I believe that our negroes are much more comfortable than workers in Britain. ❜

Now look at evidence B, C, D, E and F. Do these tell the same story about slaves in Jamaica?

B A planter's problem, 1831–32

❛ In one year I have lost twelve new negroes by dirt-eating, though I fed them well. They told me they preferred dying to living. ❜

C A runaway slave

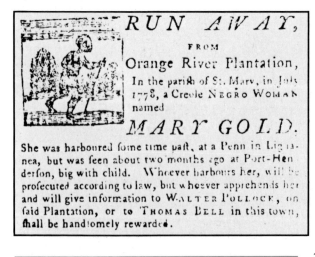

RUN AWAY,

FROM

Orange River Plantation,
In the parish of St. Mary, in July
1778, a Creole NEGRO WOMAN
named

MARY GOLD.

She was harboured some time past, at a Penn in Liguanea, but was seen about two months ago at Port-Henderson, big with child. Whoever harbours her, will be prosecuted according to law, but whoever apprehends her and will give information to WALTER POLLOCK, on said Plantation, or to THOMAS BELL in this town, shall be handsomely rewarded.

D The story of Nanny and the Maroons: a folk-tale from Jamaica

❛ In the days of slavery there were free people in Jamaica, free black people called Maroons. Some had escaped from the Spaniards, some from the English, and some were born free. They built their own little towns high in the Blue Mountains or in Cockpit country – Accompong, Maroon Town and Nanny Town. They had great leaders, the fierce Cudjoe, the cunning Quao. But first and foremost there was Nanny. Nanny was a woman and a warrior. ❜

E A photograph of Cockpit country

English soldiers called this "the land of look behind". Can you say why?

F The story of Tacky's rebellion, 1760

❛ Tacky arrived in Jamaica from West Africa with 150 other slaves in 1760. They were sent to nearby plantations. One night, not long after their arrival, Tacky organised a rebellion.

Soon after midnight, they crept out and attacked a nearby fort. They took guns and travelled inland, burning buildings and fields of cane. Slaves from other plantations soon joined them. At the same time the planters joined together to hunt the rebels.

Tacky was shot and killed in the woods. Some of the other leaders were caught alive. One rebel was burned alive in the street. Two others were hung up in the main street of Kingston and starved to death. ❜

It's your turn now

1 What differences can you see between A and the other evidence?

2 Why did the plantation owner say the slaves were happy?

3 Look at the map of Jamaica on page 20. Which clues help to prove that the story of the Maroons is true?

4 Imagine that you are one of Elizabeth's ancestors. Would you choose to (a) accept the situation, (b) run away, (c) rebel?

5 Imagine you are a planter. Explain why you punished Tacky's rebels so harshly and in the street.

13 Forgotten Africa?

The planters could not make all their captives accept slavery. But did they make them forget Africa and their old way of life?

On this page you can see some of the words, stories, beliefs and customs of people in Jamaica over the last 200 years.

• Can you link each one with a picture from Ghana and Nigeria in Africa on page 31?

Jamaica

Words

Stories

Beliefs

❝ At Christmas my mother would go to the east window of our house and pour a cup of drink outside and say, "Happy Christmas my relatives and loved ones". ❞

Customs

(*A planter's diary, 25th December 1812*)

Ghana and Nigeria

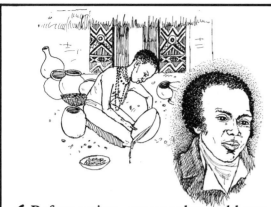

❝ Before eating, our people would put some meat and drink on the ground to thank their spirit relatives. ❞
(Olaudah Equiano)

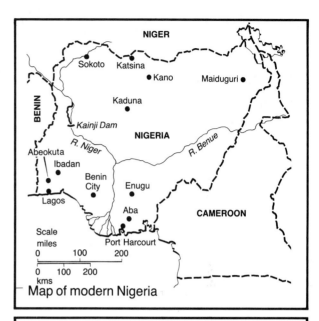

Map of modern Nigeria

❝ All our great events were celebrated with dancing, music and singing. ❞
(Olaudah Equiano)

Some words from the Twi language of Ghana

me = I
wo = you
ono = he, she, it

14 Looking back at Africa

The planters allowed their slaves to marry and have children. These children grew up without seeing Africa. But their parents would have told them about their home country, their villages and their other families.

It's your turn now

1 Imagine that you are one of Elizabeth's ancestors. You are telling your children about Africa and comparing it with your life on the plantation.
a What things in your life have changed since you left Africa?
b What things are still the same?

2 Write, draw or tape your story. The pictures on these pages will help you.

Living

Working

Deciding

Celebrating

Fighting

Believing

15 Freedom!

Celebrating Freedom Day

We do not know exactly when Elizabeth's ancestors came to the West Indies. It is too long ago for anyone to remember. But they probably arrived sometime between 1650 and 1807. The sugar planters on Jamaica began to look for African workers around 1650. Over the next 150 years European traders brought around 12 million captives from Africa to the West Indies and America.

By 1800, however, many people in Britain were trying to stop slavery. At last, in 1807, British captains were forbidden to bring any new captives from Africa. Nearly thirty years later, on 1st August 1834, all British slaves in the West Indies were set free.

Elizabeth's family now had a chance to make a better life. This was not easy. Many people did not want to carry on working in the plantations even though they would now be paid. But there were few other jobs on the islands.

It's your turn now

By the time Elizabeth's grandparents were born, her family had been living as free people in Jamaica for a hundred years.

Look at the memories and pictures on this page and the next two pages.

1 What was life like in Jamaica between 1930 and 1950?

2 What things had changed since 1834?

3 Had anything stayed the same?

Working

❝ The people grow vegetables for themselves. They grow yams, cocoa, maize and peas. They work in the fields. They work in the factory. If you can't get work you go and cut cane. ❞

❝ I have to go in the pasture in the morning, milk the cows, go in the afternoon, give them water. We didn't have no water pipes in the yard. You had to go to the river to get water in buckets. ❞

Living

❛ Life in Jamaica is one of the best life. We haven't got a lot of money but we are happy and loving people. ❜

❛ At night time, about 8 o'clock everybody close in. Especially if you live in the country. The country is always dark. Sometimes your mother start to tell you lots of stories. ❜

Celebrating

❛ We go to church on Christmas morning. Then when we come out our Mum bring lots of food – fried fish and dumplings, sorrel with white rum. Then we have fireworks, make lots of noise. ❜

❛ On emancipation day we celebrate the freeing of all the slaves in Jamaica. The main event was the church fair. Bamboo fifes and drums make the music and there were merry-go-round rides. ❜

School-days

❛ We had to walk to school. The school was about 3 miles [that's about 5 kilometres] from my home. ❜

❛ Now in the morning we must be on time for school. If we are late we think "Oh the cane again". Some children say "I don't like the cane" and away they ran. ❜

❛ My father died when I was ten years old. My mum could not send me to school because there were six of us. I had to look after the others. When I saw my friend going to school I used to cry because I wanted to go. ❜

16 Coming to Britain

Soon after slavery ended, people began to leave Jamaica to look for work. Most went to the United States of America. This was not far away so they often came home for holidays or special occasions and sent money home to support their families.

Then, in 1952, the Americans decided that only 800 people from the Caribbean could go to work in the USA each year.

So where could West Indian people find work now?

As there was a shortage of workers in Britain, British firms and the government set up job centres in Jamaica and other islands asking people to come and work in Britain. So many people, including Elizabeth's parents, decided to make the long journey to England.

WEST INDIANS ARRIVE IN BRITAIN

FROM OUR CORRESPONDENT

FOLKESTONE, MAY 1

Nearly 1,000 West Indians crossed the Channel from Calais to Folkestone to-day by the s.s. Cote d'Azur in order to find work in the United Kingdom. Most of the men were of the artisan class; a number of the young women expressed their intention of becoming nurses, but the majority of the women were dressmakers and domestic workers.

They sailed from Kingston on April 15 in an Italian ship for Genoa. From the Italian port they travelled across France in two special trains to Calais, where they embarked for England.

It's your turn now

Look at the pictures, the poem and the memories. How many differences can you spot between the journey Elizabeth's parents made to England in the 1960s and the journey their ancestors made to the West Indies 200 years earlier? Make a grid of the differences to help you.
Think about:
Reasons for leaving; preparing for the journey; type of transport; conditions on the journey; thoughts about your new country; your hopes and fears for the future.

❛ The night before we left we had a big party. All our friends and relatives came to wave us goodbye. We were happy and sad all at the same time. ❜

❛ There were adverts everywhere – "Come to the Mother country! Your Mother country needs you!". England really was our Mother country. So being away from home wouldn't be that terrible because you would belong. ❜

Colonisation in reverse
What a joyful news Miss Mattie,
I feel like me heart gwine burs.
Jamaica people colonizin
Englan in reverse.

By de hundred, by de t'ousan
From country and from town
By de ship load, by de plane load
Jamaica is Englan boun.

Dem a pour out o'Jamaica
Everybody future plan
Is fe get a big time job
An settle in de mother lan....

Louise Bennett

GO DIRECT to Plymouth
ENGLAND
aboard the POPULAR and DEPENDABLE
S.S. "AURIGA"

THE FINEST TRAVEL VALUE
available for your voyage to ENGLAND!

SAILING FOR PLYMOUTH ON
Oct. 28th
ACCOMMODATIONS NOW AVAILABLE at
£75

BOOK NOW
and be sure of your reservations ...
SEE YOUR TRAVEL AGENT TODAY
and say
"AURIGA"
Fratelli-Grimaldi Shipping Line
General Agents:
Lascelles, deMercado & Co., Ltd.

17 First thoughts

As they grew up in Jamaica, Elizabeth's parents and grandparents heard a lot about Britain. Jamaica had been ruled by Britain for almost 300 years before it became an independent country in 1944. Most Jamaican people looked on Britain as their Mother country – a second home.

But when they arrived, they were surprised by some of the things they saw and felt.

Right: Arriving in Britain

Below: At the railway station

❝ I look at the trees and I said "What's the matter with all them trees? They die? Back home trees don't drop leaves." ❞

❝ It was a cold, cold November day. People were so cold. I wanted to turn round and go back. It had all been a horrible mistake. ❞

❝ I was surprised to see English people sweeping the streets. ❞

It's your turn now

Imagine that you are Elizabeth's mother or father looking at this street for the first time.

1 Make a list of all the things that are different from Jamaica. Explain why these things are different.

2 Say how you feel about coming to England now.

18 Making a new life

Many people found that things didn't work out as they had hoped. It was a long time before they felt that they belonged. Look at the pictures and the memories.

Living

❝ It was terrible hard to find somewhere to live. As soon as they see you black, they just shut the door in your face. Sometimes they just peep through the curtains and don't come. ❞

❝ My first winter the room was so cold, thinking about it now makes me shiver. Three of us were sharing a room. We had to wash out clothes and dry them round the fire. ❞

Working

❝ My friend and I decide we would apply for a nursing job. We took a taxi to Bethnal Green hospital only to find that my friend and I wouldn't be staying together. I was to go to West Midland hospital. That was my first disappointment. ❞

❝ I went for a job. But when the manager see that I was black right away him say sorry he did not have any vacancy. ❞

❝ The first job I get, it was no good. It was 2/6 [12½p] an hour, £6.02p a week. ❞

❝ We always got the dirty jobs cleaning the machines and we were never made supervisor. ❞

Believing

‘ The church here was different. People were not happy and joyful as back home. So we set up our own church. ’

Celebrating

‘ We missed our celebration and singing and dancing. So now we arrange a carnival every year. ’

Chapeltown carnival, Leeds

Going to school

‘ At home in Jamaica I wanted to read and write properly and be a nurse or teacher. But I was sick and fell behind at school so I never got a chance. My children start school here. I want them to do well. My daughter is good at science and wants to go to college. My son likes sport and dancing. ’

It's your turn now

Imagine you are Elizabeth's father or mother.

1 You have lived in England for a year. Write a letter home telling about some of the problems that you have faced.

2 You have lived in England for ten years now. Write a letter to your relatives in Jamaica saying what you have done to make yourself feel more at home.

19 Looking back at changes

Over the last 200 years or so, Elizabeth's family have travelled across the world and made a new life in two different countries. Each time some parts of their life changed. But some parts stayed the same. When things continue as they were before, we call it *continuity*.

Look at the pictures. They show Elizabeth's family at different times and in different places.

1 Which parts of their lives changed most over the years?

2 When did these changes happen and why?

3 Which parts of their lives stayed the same?

4 Can you suggest any reason for this continuity?

5 Think about other aspects of life like *believing or talking*.
   a Did these aspects change or continue as Elizabeth's family moved from West Africa to the West Indies and to West Yorkshire?
   b Try to give reasons for these changes or continuities.

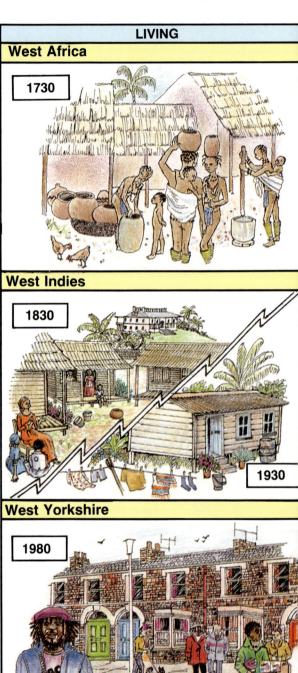

LIVING

West Africa

1730

West Indies

1830

1930

West Yorkshire

1980

WORKING	CELEBRATING

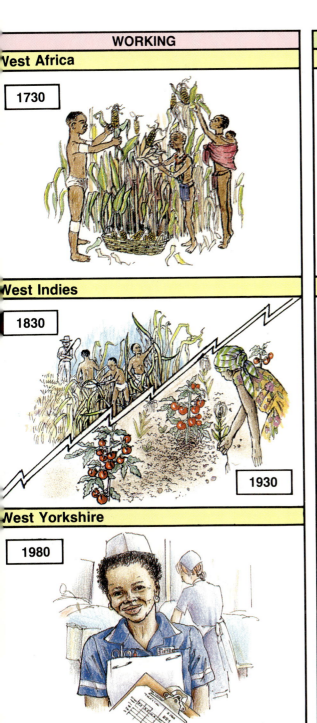

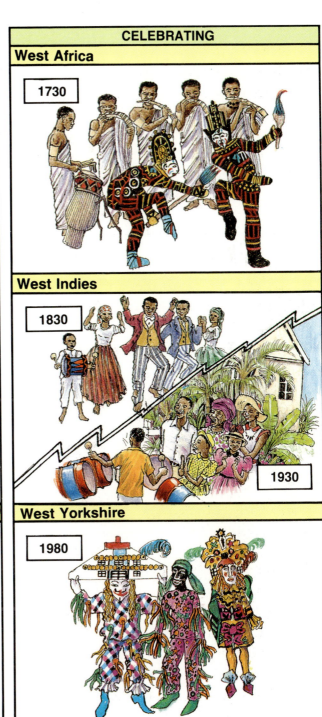

West Africa
1730

West Indies
1830
1930

West Yorkshire
1980

20 Why did they do it?

In your investigations you have found out about:

- the journeys made by Elizabeth's family;
- the reasons they made these journeys;
- their hopes and fears on the journeys;
- what happened when they arrived.

Working out why people do things (their *motives*) is not simple. Sometimes their motives are easy for us to understand, sometimes they are hard.

People may choose to do something or they may be forced into it. Often it's a bit of both. Even when people choose to do something, they cannot be sure how things will work out in the end.

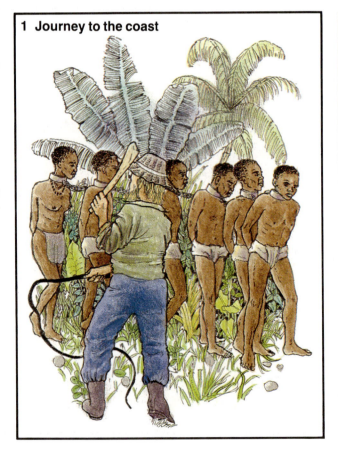

1 Journey to the coast

2 Journey to the West Indies

It's your turn now

On these pages you can see pictures of four important events that changed the lives of Elizabeth's family.

First look at these events through their eyes.

1 a Explain why you made the three journeys. Did you choose to go or were you forced to go?

 b Did things turn out as you hoped or feared?

2 Explain why you rebelled against the plantation owner.

Now look at these events through different eyes.

3 Imagine you were an African king. Why did you sell Africans to European slave traders?

4 Imagine you were a captain of a slave ship. Why did you not treat your captives better?

5 Imagine you were a planter. Why did you not give your slaves more freedom?

6 Imagine you were an English workmate. Why didn't you make Elizabeth's parents more welcome?

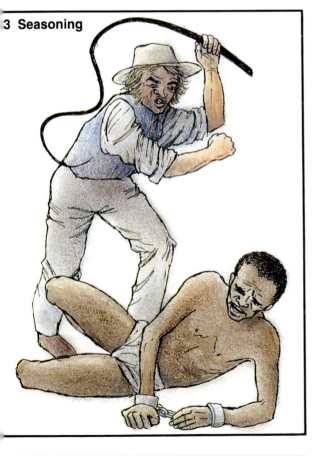

3 Seasoning

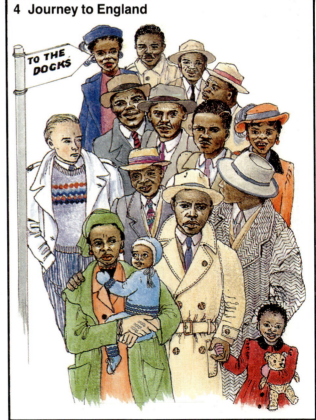

4 Journey to England

TO THE DOCKS

Acknowledgements

The author and publishers wish to acknowledge the following photograph sources:

BBC Hulton Picture Library, pages 14 (top), 40 (bottom); Anne Bolt, pages 5 (bottom left), 35; Jim Brownbill, page 5 (centre); Camera Press, page 29; J Allan Cash, page 3; Mary Evans Picture Library, pages 14 (bottom), 25 (top right); Mansell Collection, pages 13, 34; Popperfoto, pages 5 (centre bottom), 40 (top); Royal Commonwealth Society, pages 25, 27 (top left); John Topham Picture Library, pages 37, 43 (top left); By kind permission of the Trustees of the Wedgwood Museum, Barleston, page 17;

Cover photograph Popperfoto

The publishers have made every effort to trace all the copyright holders, but where they have failed to do so they will be pleased to make the necessary arrangements at the first opportunity.

First published 1988

Published by
MACMILLAN EDUCATION LTD
Houndmills, Basingstoke, Hampshire RG21 2XS
and London
Companies and representatives
throughout the world

Illustrated by Ursula Seiger
Maps by Illustra Design
Cover illustration Gabrielle Stoddart
Designed by Sylvia Tate

Printed in Hong Kong

British Library Cataloguing in Publication Data
Gwyn, Carole,
Elizabeth's Story. —(Time Detectives; Bk.4.)
1. Slaves—Jamaica—History—19th century
2. Blacks—Jamaica—History—19th century
I. Title   II. Series
305.5′67′097292   HT1096
ISBN 0–333–38843–7